New Poetry

James Walmsley

Published by New Generation Publishing in 2019

First Edition

ISBN: 978-1-78955-876-0

www.newgeneration-publishing.com

Words

If I had words the world could see
What perfect things we all could be
All the badness through the days
And the suffering at our feet it lays.

Sadness comes in the dead of night
Remembered scenes of satans bite
Played in tableau mankind's plight
Laid before us is evils rite.

As the sunlight caresses the dawn
A new day for all is but born
But for some the sun will not shine
Another day, a life riven and torn.

We have no wand that we can wave
There is no magic that can save
All there is, is you and me
And our words to help people see.

If I had words the word cold see
What a world this could be
And if these words I could share
All the people might just care.

A Soldiers Story

I am just another body sleeping in the street.
Who was once a son a husband and dad.
Now just a bum dreaming about things I once had.
In another time in another place I stood erect to the bugles call, I served my country and pledged my allegiance to one and all, just to end up on the dole.
Our boys, Our boys shouted one and all.
Fuck Sadam, we sang as we marched, the crowds cheered and the church bells rang, in twelve hours time we would be knee deep in sand thinking about living and dying in a foreign land.
The war was always going to be won, it was just how and at what cost. They didn't give a shit about soldiers lost.
They never did in any war the caused.
The craven bastards told us how to die for Queen and Country whilst they lied about why.
When victory came in the glare of the press they forgot about us and our Post Traumatic Stress.
Wrapped in cardboard and rags freezing in a doorway where I do lie wondering why it is I do die.

Footsteps In The Snow

As I tread through snow so deep I wonder who I might meet.
Could it be a Wolf, that would make my heart beat. Could it
be a friend I could give a helping hand, could it be a stranger
who would join our merry band.
We could walk on together and when we sit and rest we could
talk about who we are and what we like best. I had a family once.
My wife the good lord took her and my daughter she has gone.
I pray the Good Lord will give me hope to find her for in truth I
have none.
The friend would talk about his sad life and the things he never
had. That he knew a place where no one was ever sad and they
could have everything they never had. I must admit I was tempted
but on my knees I would pray for the strength to carry on one more
day.
The stranger he would sit quietly and with a gentle smile he would
say, ‘ we cannot choose who we are, we can choose what we are.
There are two paths in this life, the good and the bad, the choice is
yours to make.
The friend he will leave us for he is the Wolf, as for you, you have hope
all you need is faith.
The stranger said he would walk with me for a while, after a mile or so
I turned to the friend, he was nowhere to be seen. The stranger said he
will tempt you no more because down this path he has never been.
There's a cottage up ahead knock on the door and ask for shelter, it's
my birthday today it would be nice to be warm on my birthday.

Footsteps in the snow Continued

In the cottage a young man sat at a table with a child the floor was covered in wrapping paper and presents a beautifully decorated Christmas tree was stood in the corner. It was an happy place.
There was a knock, the young man opened the door and there before him was an elderly man, covered in sno,' can we come in and shelter in the warm for a while, it's bitterly cold, we will soon be on our way. 'We said the young man, yes me and my companion; I meet hum on the road, well, said the young man there are only one set of footprints in the snow and they're yours, but come in and get war. This is our daughter Gracie, the old man looked at her oddly.
Then a voice that sounded like it had passed through the lips of an Angel said please stay and celebrate the birth of the Lord for today is Christmas Day.
The man turned his head and framed in the doorway was the image or his Wife Grace. He fell on his knees and wept for he knew before him was his long lost daughter. And finally he understood.

Life

On my travels through this life I gave seen so many things.
I see the sun rise every day and the miracle of life it brings.
The path I take upon this earth is entirely down to me.
And down that path I see how beautiful life can be.
To watch a flower petals open is wondrous for me to me.
And to here the birds sing there perfect symphonies .
A child's scream of pleasure as they play in the park.
A loving arm around a friend to heal a broken heart.
To walk with your love hand in hand.
Through the garden and knowing that you will never part.
And then it happens another beating heart.
And if I have ever loved I never loved like I loved on that
Given day.
And in the Autumn of my life I stand with my love my wife.
We look down at another beating heart our grandchild.
And if we have ever loved we have never loved.
Like we loved on that given day.

Dog talk

I've got a little dog and he really likes to talk, no you don't
believe me, so let me tell you this is no joke.
It started on a Sunday when on our morning walk, we bumpedk
Into Peggy and her French Poodle Nicole.
She was very dig with hair as black coal, Alfie did not like her
much because he was only ten inch tall. As we stopped to listen
to all of Peggy's woes.
Alfie just stood there tapping one of his paws.
The poodle ran in circles chasing what only Nicole knows.
Alfie just sat there tapping one of his paws.
Peggy said she had, had a little bit of a tadoo, Nicole went
next door and left a big poo, but do you know that is
somewhere that Nicole goes.
Alfie just sat there tapping one of his paws.
Peggy said she had hurt her leg how she didn't say, she
Said she was very sore and she had rubbed the bugger raw.
Alfie just sat there tapping one of his paws.
Eventually Peggy ambled off with Nicole in close pursuit.
I watched her go to where the old oak tree grows,
Alfie just set there just tapping one of his paws.
I really love you Alfie I love you best of all .
'Oh for heavens sake woman, just throw the bloody ball.

The Christening

I wonder why we sometimes cry
Happy is my house today
I have searched every nook and cranny
A dry eye I have not found any
It’s a Christening today
The church bells will ring
The tears will role, the baby will ball
And then we will all have to sing
The tearful vicar will shake our hands
And hope for twenty nicker
It's the roof you know
Then off to the pub he will go
Grandad makes a speech with a big grin
Grandma drowning in tears and gin
And the baby is still balling
Grandma slips the vicar trips
And carnage is unfolding
There were knickers and suspenders
All in colourful hue
And Grandma’s were on show too
The vicar had surely missed his calling
And the baby just went on balling
The music had stopped the day is done
The vicar is sleeping, Grandma's happy
As for Grandad.
He's changing the babies nappy.

The Seven Deadly Sins

The seven deadly sins are all self indulgent
They have no real relevance to mankind
you see they really are redundant.
Pride is not a sin there has never been
a man or god who has not been proud
of his beautiful wife.
A poor man cannot go to heaven because
Envy is one of the seven.
Gluttony today just means you are ill the
Doctor will say you're depressed and issue
you with a pill.
Sloth lazy and feckless the bosses vent.
They don't pay us enough to pay the
sodding rent.
Wrath what can you do when they take
your money, you're disabled, sat there
in a daze which soon evolves into
uncontrollable rage.
Greed the rich take what they don't need
from the poor no matter what colour or creed.
Procreation is why we are here, we seal the
deal with Lust it's an absolute must.

The Courier

He walks through the desolate street in the pouring rain,
He knows he cannot be late or he will feel the pain.
He is the man of the house his father is gone.
His mother she drinks and uses, hope she has none.
He works all night and most of the day. he's a County Line
Courier and must do what they say.

Over to Camden Town to pick up the gear, into the stash
house to see Billy the Queer. Careful not to say the wrong
thing or show him any fear.
He picked up the package and began to check, he could feel
Billy the Queer's breath on the nape of his neck.
It's all there you little shit you don't have to look.
But Billy was a user, you could tell the way he shook.

Down to the Crescent to catch the tube, on the Northern line
business to conclude. Half a key to go over the line, keep your
cool everything will be fine. Make the meet with Sour Face,
pass him the snow and it's off we go. On the tube back down
to Town over to the stash house to pick up the brown.
Picked up by Bixie on the back of his scooter, don't piss him
Off he's got a shooter.

Next day pick up my pay, that's what it's all about, not much more
to say. Got the call to meet the boss, bit of a drag to Brent Cross.
Get off the tube, meet Sour Face and Bixie in the carpark, we'll
have a doss.
He walked into the carpark, they came out of the dark.
The Courier continued.
A woman found him, she head a shout, he was slumped by a wall
where he had managed to crawl. She called for an ambulance it was
to late he had bled out.
The policeman asked if he spoke before he died, Yes ,he said,
" they said I had been skimming the coke, then they stabbed
me and left me here. but it wasn't me it was Billy the Queer.

The Visitor

The visitor was silent, invisible looking down.
Ousing malice feeding on despair.
His spiteful breath corrupting the air.
She was just thirteen now crooked smashed.
Once vital once loved, now a pariah an outcast.
Fading memories of a long lost past.
Battered, bruised living a life just used abused.
He offered love only with a laughing smile.
His soul was full of venom and putrid bile.
He gave happiness only crack can feign.
Sold to the highest bidder again and again.
She lay on her back her eyes wide open.
Still just a child dead and broken.
He walked through the door without a care.
His spiteful breath corrupting the air.

The Question

If your god was a man what kind of god would he be.
Would he be the god of peace or would it war he would unleash.
Would he be the god of love or would he be the god of hate.
Would he be the god to suffer or the god who would forsake.
Would he be the god who is causing global warming.
Or would it man ignoring the planets warning.
Could it be that god is vainglorious a figment of man's mind.
Could it be just a way to subjugate mankind.
In all the places man has lived and built a life to share.
In all the death and tragedies there has been.
God caring hand has never been seen.
For the will of god is a figment to appease some men's guilty minds
If god was god and not a figment of man's mind and it was gods will.
Then there is no hope for mankind.

Torment

I am alien to the pain of this world.
I watch the epic slide with total disdain.
The greedy steal from the needy and laugh.
Men beat up on women and woman beat
up on themselves.
We never learn we only obey the want to
take the want to lust.
We fight and squabble over a patch of dust,
because we must.
It’s our way to be giver of pain, self inflicted
It's all the same,
And when it's time we like to cry and when
It's time we like to deny.
Now is night tomorrow is day all the suffering
Will go in a box, it's always been that way.
That’s the paradox.

Should

Should I be wrong about how people feel.
Some say they are but a number not real.
Should I be wrong to say that some people
are of no consequence to people in power.
Should I be wrong to say that some people
Pray to a non-existent god to save their souls.
Should I be wrong to say that some people deny
their gods grace to people who are fleeing just
because of their race.
Should I be wrong to say don't stand by or turn
away the children when their only alternative is
to die.
Should I be wrong to say that gods good grace is
just another lie.

Contentment

Suddenly it seemed it stopped,
it wasn't a dreams somewhat unreal surreal.
A new beginning a new birth, all the same things
all the same people the same visage but the pain,
the pain had gone.
Contentment..
Has always been elusive hidden as it is in some
Imagined place.
Where there are no doubts, no tears no pain.
A place with only one door one key, once there
the key is gone the door no more.
All there is in this place is everything you have
ever wanted in that one word.
Contentment..
To sit and smile at all around you, wonder at the
beauty that astounds you.
To feel love and warmth floating on a cushion of
Contentment..
Never a tear, never a shout never a doubt, all the
trouble all the strife, all the rage, all the pain and
resentment, a life spent looking for
Contentment..
Why?
When all I have to do is die.

Oppression

So many people about, no guilt no contrition.
The evil beginning to rise, manifesting before
Our very eyes.
History lessons still not leaned, heads turned
looking in shop windows as half the world
begins to burn.

The murdered forests, the giver of life,
polluted rivers foul air.
Political meltdown all over the world, mad men
reaping souls turning cities into gapping holes.

The children of the world are crying.
As evil takes as evil wants.
Whilst we look in shop windows denying.
The children of the world are dying.

Look into your child's eyes and see your
Grandchildren that might never be
Turn away from the shop window and look.
Raise your consciousness and see your
Grandchildren the evil never took.

The Martyr

As the rain lashes down it scours my very soul.
Memories scraping through my mind causing pain.
Yet I endure.
I hang on to last vestige of my sanity all hope gone.
Thoughts of a place no longer relevant a home no
longer there.
Memories of homes destroyed, broken promises.
Forgotten people, death rotting corpses.
Flashing images of a half remembered time.
What are the, who are they where are they.
Children, walk endlessly through my mind.
Looking for love, looking for a mother, no longer,
a home no longer, hope no longer. Once a dream a new
beginning. Give yourself all of yourself, yield unto me and I
will give.
I will show you the path to a better way, walk with me
and give yourself wholly to me.
I will give you silver, gold and beauty untold.
I will lead you from the dark.
I will show you the light.
I will show you the way.
I will show you paradise
The rain has stopped the sun now scorches my soul.
The voice lifts into the now, pushed and prodded I walk
hands bound.
The scaffold, just a shimmer, surreal it waits patiently.
The rope around my neck, the voice says Jahannam for you
Then nothing.
,On This Day All Gods Died.
It seemed a nice place, tranquil the surf breaking.
The red hot sun low in the West. A ship at anchor,
Black against the setting sun. Boats being rowed
Towards the shore for cargo.

The boy watched the small antelope as it turned
Its head sniffed the air and bolted. He saw his
anticipated feast disappear into the bush perhaps
another day Ishwalanda thought. I must remember
the hunt, he turned and walked towards the village
by the ocean.

The boats reached the shore and the smell reached the boats. The oarsmen just stared at what lay before them. What lay before them was beaten and broken humanity tethered and shackled, in lines that filled the beach. The whips cracked and the first line shuffled towards the boats, the coarse voices shouting the whips slashing flesh and bone.

Ishwalanda could smell the fire, a feral smell a smell that he would remember for the rest of his years. The village was burning, empty except for the very old. The old man Who chased the children away lay dead; war club in hand.

The boats carried twenty, they walked in single file towards them one by one they were dragged aboard and taken to the ship, herded like cattle taken to the slave decks and shackled head to toe. Twelve hundred were crammed aboard just over
On This Day All Gods Died.
Continued.
One third would survive the voyage.
Ishwalanda followed the tracks of humanity down to the ocean always a sickly sweet smell in the air. He looked down the beach, nothing but sea sand and silence.

The ship hauled anchor set sail and headed West, all that could be heard was the sound of the sea and the moan of its cargo as it cried. The master prayed for a fair passage, but to no avail, because on this day all gods died.

Ishwalanda saw the ship sail beyond the headland with his people on board. Tears streaming down his cheeks he turned waked into the bush where he wept and three hundred years later Ishwalanda is still weeping.

Step After Step

Through the biting wind head bowed, never a minutes
peace from its relentless assault.
Mordant etching lines across the face of hope, then the
rain it drenches fully, it has no adversaries, it has no pain
no feeling, the weak fall by the wayside.
Step After Step.
Away from hell, away from hate barrel bombs and bullets.
The landscape riven with the dying and the dead.
Bombed out corrupted by war, broken trees smashed houses.
Just men with guns, stray dogs looking for food; being food.
Step After Step.
Tasting the stench of rotting corpses , then rats a writhing screeching
mass of flesh eating horror.
The night shrouds the macabre tableau played out every day.
All that is left is the capuff of distant air raids and the abject
fear of crying children.
Step After Step.
The misery moves on, mile after mile to find humanity to be
human.
When they came to our mountains we gave them food and shelter.
They took our food and our shelter. Then they took our land, our
Homes, our children and then our lives. What is left is this line of
bedraggled starving humanity.
Step After Step.
Through the desert heat, left behind the desecrated remains of
our mountain home, abandoned by god abandoned by the world.
Step After Step.
We are less everyday.
Continued
Step After Step.
Into the camps we will go
Step After Step.
Where we will stay.
Step After Step.
Until we fade away.

Drunk

I say to you why did you leave me here.
What am I, what is it you want me to do.
I am nowhere I am no one I depend on you.
Standing on a dirty wet street hoping for
some goodness, but all there is, is the rains
relentless beat.
The passing pass without a thought all they
leave is the fading patter of feet as they head
for their homes so neat.
There was a time in another place before I fell
from grace that I had the "needs" that anyone
could ever need and I would have passed with
the passing.
You punish me for thing I did, you make me walk
from street to street just to find a morel I could
eat.
You send your legions of wind and rain to torture
my soul but my maker you will not let us meet.
I remember the smell of the dead and dying.
I remember the horror the smell tells.
I remember the bottle and the cells.
I remember my family and the bottle.
I remember the church and the bottle.
I forgot my family but not the bottle.

Drunk continued

And in this doorway where I lie even sleep for me
you deny
In the recess of my mind you come mocking.
Dangling portraits of laughter and reminiscences
turning into shocking grimaces.
It pleases you to tell how they died.
And the carnage you vividly describe,
And the alcohol imbibed.
You tell me I was thrown from the car.
You laugh when I asked you why.
Drunk you said as you watched my children die.

The Adventures Of Sir Useless Cockupalot

There was a knight of old who was ever so bald but you
have never heard of him because his story has never
been told.
His name was Sir Useless Cockupalot he was one of
King Arthur's Knights, he was called so bald because
he didn't have a hair on his head.
Useless was the progeny of Sir Lancelot of the Lake
And the barmaid at the Heaven's Above Tavern
Lucy Likecock; and often, they would meet in the
stable and there they would procreate at a hell of
A rate that would make the building shake.
Useless first came to the notice of King Arthur
at the battle of Stinking Meadow as it would
become known.
Thirty thousand Picts came from the North to
plunder and pillage and this they did to every
village.
Arthur's army gathered all Knights of the Round
Table and anyone else who was able.
Dig the latrines said Lancelot to Useless, dig them
wide and dig them deep and this is what our hero
did; sort of.
He got his spade and a ditch he made.
Day after day he toiled excavating the soil, did our
Useless with selfless pride and an enormous smile.
By the time it was finished it stretched for half mile.
As the army passed on its way for a crap they all gave
Continued
Useless a pat on the back.
Well after a month the ditch was full to steaming,
everyone's eyes were streaming.
And when the Picts did finally appear, yes you have
Guessed it, it was in the rear, the cry went out they're
here they're here they're in the rear.
Our hero lit a torch for a bit of light, took one look then
took flight throwing the torch high into the night it
Landed right into the middle of the shite .
The gas ignited then it blew and thirty thousand Picts
were covered in shit,
And Useless had won the day.

For M.L.W

If ever there the was a majestic beauty
A beauty that truly astounds
Where such things abound
A beauty to compare
To beauty that ever were
And if I was so profound
To compound all the beauty I have found
I am bound to think of you.

I am Jew nor Gentile
I am my fathers son
I am the smile on my mothers face
I am the hope that are my children
All I have to offer is life love and peace
All I have said is true
I am Jew nor Gentile
I am you.

The Margins Of My Mind

As I walk down this worried path
Where many a man and beast have tread
Pondered the life I do hath
Wonder at what was weaved by life's thread.

Regret is in the margins of my mind
For regret is not a thing of the unselfish
It is a thought that is always unkind
And just a thought that is here to punish.

Walking with my father when just a boy
Whose thread of life is not yet weaved
With a fertile mind ready for the seed
That some men are ready to deceive.

The fork in the path is up ahead
Like all forks it offers choice
The boy will choose in his fathers stead
Striven to remember his fathers voice.

And if the path he walks is full of turns
Demons plague him and point the way
At this time for his father he yearns
For just a hint of where the right path lay.

When the path runs straight and true
And when there is little else to do
No longer driven to achieve
Still there are those who would deceive.

Where Fathers Fish And Mothers Smile

The river meanders on its way to the sea
Past meadow and wood hamlet and lea
This sliver of silver in silence it flows
What secrets it hides no one knows.

The places it passes are mans creation
Homes to live love and flourish
Village and town to forge a nation
Fertile land for man to nourish.

When the rains come and the wind blows
The river fills and man stands in awe
It comes with a rush and a mighty roar
And the silver river is silent no more.

Through the days months and years
The silver river ebbs and flows
In its midst it carries all mankind's tears
And in its wake the country grows.

In the beginning of all mankind
And in the valley of creation
There the ties where made that bind
And all mankind became one nation.

On the banks the children play
As the silver river runs on its way
As Fathers Fish and Mothers Smile
They give thanks to the mighty Nile.

The Crowded City
(The London Bridge Attack)

Its nearly midnight in the crowded
They walked hand in hand as lovers do
Seeing no one in their loves intensity
A love for each other a love so true.

To young people with a life to live
A loving smile and a loving kiss
The wonder at what life has to give
A future together a future of bliss.

Through the streets of neon light
The lovers in awe of the surreal sight
Now arm in arm into the night
Yet to feel all of satans spite.

Cross the road onto the bridge of fate
Right into the teeth of satans hate
Is this the path of death they take
Or is it fates decision to make.

In the crowded city in the dead of night
Hatred is once again mankind's blight
The lovers are safe in gods embrace
And continue to live in gods good grace.

Black Savage

The Beginning - Part 1

In the wildest of winds on the darkest of nights she lies beneath the Northern Lights.
The time has come for her to birth her foal, so beautiful the colour of coal.
Black Savage he would come to be known, when he is fully grown but for now
he must stay where he lay, she will help him survive his very first day.
In the spring the prairie sings of life that nature brings. Grasses grow Eagles
soar and little mice, well they just gnaw. The Buffalo graze in a misty haze as they
wander in a bovine daze.
Black Savage is just six months old straight of back and strong and bold. He struts
thorough herd with his nostrils flared, there to be challenged if anything dared.
By the river there was a place that few thing knew, a village the home of the Lakota Sioux, and there lived a boy strong and tall ready to answer the warrior
call.
He followed the river as it courses on his quest to find wild horses. Across the plains
for days he trekked past the village the invaders had wrecked. He looked to the sky
and shouted, I am strong and tall and on my knees I vow to thee, to avenge the mighty-
Cree. It was the boy who had spoken in the dawn it was the man who had awoken.

The Bond - Part 2

The old stallion stopped and bowed his head, he looked around at the herd he led.
One thousand strong all mustang bred into the hills and through the canyon led the
old stallion. On they went to the end of the day to a place he knew he would have to
stay.

On the hill stands a man, he watches with piercing eyes, he sees the old stallion stumble
and die. The herd is lost a river to cross no leader to heed, nervous ready to stampede.
All at once the herd parted from its midst a beast, with a wild eye it looked to the East
and there if saw a man, it stared and snorted turned its head and off it led one thousand
horses to be watered and fed.
He slept upon the hill, the night was eerily still. He dreamed the dream of things to
come, he dreamed about the invaders might he dreamed about the coming fight but the
dream he remembered was not of the invaders might nor the coming fight. It was the
magnificent sight of a horse as black as night walking through the herd to make his stand
and take command.
He stood again upon the hill, he touched the hemp around his waist and off he went to
Join the chase to catch a horse his war horse. Three days he tracked the herd never seen
but often heard.
On the fourth day he saw a smear in the sky, he felt a tinge of fear and he was sure he
knew why. He headed in the direction of the smoke, just before sunset on a breath of wind
he heard the patter of talk. He waited for the light to go then crept up to the top of the draw
and there below in the campfire glow were his enemy the Crow.
The black colt was hobbled and sore, tied to a tree impossible for him to break free.
He waited until the fire died and worked his way around the other side. On his hands and
knees he crawled, he drew his knife and cut the hobble, he stood upright by the tree to enable
the wild eyed colt to see. He uncoiled the hemp from around his waist and placed it over the
colts head and then the horse he led. They walked together man and beast for ever travelling
East the journey long, he treat his wounds the colt was strong and there the bond was made.

The Battle Of Little Bighorn - Part 3

1876

Seven thousand some have said the day the prairie bled. Sioux, Cheyanne, Arapaho and Cree.
The first attack came just after three. The invaders one hundred strong fired into the throng,
the warriors held then they yelled and drove them into the trees.
They met in the big lodge, war chiefs all, Sitting Bull, Dull Knife, Crazy Horse and Lone Wolf.
And there the planned what would become known as Custers Last Stand.
He mounted Black Savage war club in hand, he quietly said On Black Savage On he knew his evert command. They galloped away the finest light cavalry of its day, every warrior sworn to follow, so off they went into the trees and there they routed the enemy force, led by the great Sioux war chief Crazy Horse.
He walked Black Savage to the river, they both drank, he washed his war club running red with
enemy dead. He mounted black Savage and quietly said, On Black Savage On.
The fighting moved from hill to hill, the dying cried and the dead were for ever still. The warriors took cover in the folds of the land, the invaders atop had the upper hand. They rained
down death with indifferent savagery, these were the men of the 7th Cavalry.
Crazy Horse came from the West twenty warriors mounted and lanced they charged up hill in rapid advance, the invaders numbers were slowly depleted. The warriors below took their chance, the invaders retreated.
They formed up on Custer Hill, every man knew they were defeated.
The end was fast the end was savage and men talk of the absolute carnage.
They walked down from the ridge exhausted, off the twenty warriors who charged the hill only seven remained the rest were dead dying or maimed.
In the camp by the river the people cheered and shouted, some were crying. The warriors were drunk on war and victory. Seven mounted warriors approached all blooded and black. Crazy Horse dismounted and walked to the elders and he recounted. The invaders have lost today but the are not defeated, prepare.
He turned away and looked to the sky and said I have honoured my vow to thee the mighty Cree.
He walked to his horse with a war chiefs carriage mounted and quietly said On Black Savage On.

Footnote : Crazy Horse was hunted down and captured. He was held captive at Fort Robinson in Nebraska. On the 5th of September 1877 he was murdered in his cell. Cause of death bayonet wound.
Black Savage is a figment of my imagination

The Silver Grace

Gone is the day of the sheeted mast,
Sail ships a thing of the past ,
Memories fade of voyages made,
Through oceans vast and currents fast,
Into the wind a storm to outlast.

Four points to starboard heading due West,
Now she swoons she's doing her best,
But yet to face her greatest test,
Land ahoy shouts a voice from the nest
One hundred feet above the rest.

Howling and screeching the tempest grows,
Into its teeth she boldly goes,
As if her fate it already knows,
Towards the rocks the wind it blows,
A seduction like poets prose.

The helmsman fights to turn the wheel,
The ships fate the rage will seal,
The Captain mutters a prayer an appeal,
Then the Captain he dost kneel,
To his god he makes one last deal.

The cruel sea rips like thunder,
All aboard are thrown asunder,
Now is the time for her to go under,
For the sea to claim its plunder,
Then all was calm in miraculous wonder

All was silent the wind abated,
Thirty four souls the manifest related,
All were saved but one was fated,
The Captain as the deal stated,
The cruel sea at last was sated.

The Haunting Of McDuff

On a moonlit night atop the cliffs of Clo Mor
He waits for the call of his love the Beautiful
Lady Annalise. She will come from the waves
to beckon her love to join her in here watery
grave.
On the morning of Culloden Eve she left these
shores to mourn McDuff, to be martyred for
the Jacobean cause, his ashes to be scattered
on the breeze lamented.
The Beautiful Lady Annalise.
She sailed away into the Atlantic storm a
pitiless sea would take the ship in its grip.
The sea would swallow the ship with ease
And so was the demise of
The Beautiful Lady Annalise.
On Culloden day the Mcduff's gathered to
fight, with his Claymore in hand he shouted
for Scotland, the Bonny Prince and his love
The Beautiful Lady Annalise.
The English came and slaughtered the Scots
but McDuff he lived and walked away
to take advantage of gods reprieve, to
find his love
The Beautiful Lady Annalise.
In mountain and Glen he hid, Chieftain of
his Clan Laird of the Highlands the Lord
McDuff. And there he prayed on his knees
for word of his love
The Beautiful Lady Annalise.
Then a messenger came along the path the
letter McDuff did gratefully receive. It told
of a shipwreck off Cape Wrath, as he read
the list of those at rest in utter disbelief he
saw the name of his love
The Beautiful Lady Annalise.
As the months and years passed he would
walk atop of Clo Mor stare along the coast
of Wester Ross to Cape Wrath and mourn
His love loss
The Beautiful Lady Annalise.

And then one Hallowed Eve he heard a
whisper on the breeze and this he knew
he had to concede was the call of his love
The Beautiful Lady Annalise.

He walked atop of Clo Mor once again
He heard the call and walked to the edge
and this he knew his love it would please.
There he took the hand of his love the
Beautiful Lady Annalise

In the morning of the day we now call
Halloween McDuff was found upon the
rocks below Clo Mor, his spirit had been
scattered on the breeze to spend eternity
with his love the beautiful Lady Annalise.
And if you go atop Clo Mor on the coast
of Wester Ross on a moonlit Halloween.
You might just see walking arm in arm
McDuff and his love
The Beautiful Lady Annalise.

Eternity

If I was ever to walk with you through the trick of time.

To a place where blossoms grow and lovers love.

To a tranquillity that calms my mind and caresses my heart.

And if I was to turn and gaze into the mystery of your eyes.

To wonder at the fathomless beauty I behold.

And there to love you as no other loved you.

And you to love me as no other loved me.

If this place was not a trick time but a thing of dreams.

I would dream for eternity just to be with you.

I would dream for eternity just for your touch.

I would dream for eternity just for your kiss.

I would dream for eternity just for your love.

And if this trick of time was just a trick of my mind.

I would dream this dream until the end of the time.

The Butcher

The howl of wind and the fall of leaves
As darkness shrouds this Hallowed Eve
Scraping the knife across the stone
Making sure it will slash to the bone.
The crooked smile in the broken mirror
The whetted blade ready to deliver
Out tonight looking for a throat to cut
Jack is back and he will rip and gut.

He silently walks in the dark of night
His blade reflects the pale moonlight
His heart is black his eyes are dead
His only wish is to sever a head.

He saw her blond hair, then her face
He watched her walk so full of grace
His heart beating he quickened his pace
His mind was racing he loved the chase.

She turned the corner and entered a shop
This he knew would be her last stop
He touched the blade with a smile
He knew his work would take a while.

He quietly opened then closed the door
He knew exactly where she would go
He carried the body to the bench
He slit it open and gagged at the stench.

Cutting and chopping he dismembered
Just as thrilling as he remembered
The door burst open and up Jack looked
The policeman saw the head of the hook.

He looked at the blood and the gore
He could not believe what he saw
Bit of bodies all in rows
What bits they were only Jack knows.

The blonde walked in from the flat
She looked at Jack and the offal sack
The policeman looked at the blonde
And the blonde looked back

I've just popped in and I'm glad I did
I saw you working on that lovely pig
sorry I can't stay I would love to talk
But could I some of your lovely pork.

Why Did You Leave Me So

She paces the widows walk everyday at one
a forlorn look upon her face all hope nearly gone
She yearns for just a sight of a silver sail.
She stares out sea for hours on end but it's to no avail.
She wipes a tear and stifles a cry and says,
Oh why my love
Oh why my love
Why did you leave me so
Oh why my love
Oh why my love did you ever go
The ship sailed on the one O'clock tide.
The sailor waved to his beautiful bride.
Every day she would stand and stare.
The gentle breeze would caress her hair.
Oh my love where could you be.
Oh my love please sail back to me.
The sailor stood upon the deck
Not yet knowing his ship was to be a wreck
Oh my beautiful bride I miss you so much
Oh my beautiful wife I miss your gentle touch.
Around Good Hope the ship is bound,
The ship was never found.
Last known position was off the Cape of Good Hope
September 1861.
She paces the widows walk everyday at one.
A forlorn look upon her face, all hope nearly gone,
She yearns for just a sight of a silver sail,
She stares out to sea for hours on end all to no avail,
She wipes a tear and stifles a cry and says
Oh why my love
Oh why my love
Why did you leave me so
Oh why my love
Oh why my love did you ever go.
The man watched the woman pace.
So beautiful so full of grace.
She Wiped a tear and stifles a cry.
He wrote in his book.
The most beautiful woman I have ever seen.
10th of September 2018.

A Day In the life of Bartholomew Wicks

Dirty streets full of coal dust and grime,
Scurrying hurrying to get to the mill on time,
A long day six in the morning until six at night.
Watching the shuttle as it weft the warp.

Cleaning the looms and winding machines.
Coughing up cotton dust then dodging the beam.
Don't get trapped no one will hear your scream.
Picking shafts and clattering frames.
Assaulting and battering the workers brains.

The Weavers weave and the Doffers pick.
The Winders wind the Beamgaiter give the
Scavenger a kick and off he goes to do his trick.
Under the frame to pick up the thread.
Timing the beam and ducking his head.
Listening carefully to what the Beamgaiter said.

Four thirty the whistle blew the engine stopped.
The Beamgaiter stood in absolute dread.
The beam had crushed the Scavenger dead.
The Scavenger was buried in his Sunday best.
The Beamgaiter cried as he laid his son to rest.
On the grave the inscription read.

Hear lies Bartholomew Wicks
A Beamgaiters Scavenger
Not Yet Six

Only A Tear

It's only a tear you can wipe it away,
Not like a memory that's here to stay,
It's not on its own there is also regret,
And a guilt that won't let you forget,
Choice has been made, people are hurt,
What was before is now no more.
Now you think you're nothing but dirt,

The past has been burned
All that is left is a heart that yearns.
An empty house two lives that are broken.
A thousand words left unspoken.
Never again will you be as one.
Words of love you will never hear.
All that is left is one last tear.

My heart is yours because yours is broken.
I give you my tears because yours have been shed.
I give you my words because yours have been spoken.
I give you my love to help you mend.
I give all I have to you my loving friend.

The Lonely Path

A lonely flower in a garden full of weeds.
Wandering through the blinding mist.
Following the path wherever it leads.
Not knowing why, desperation insists.

My way is long and hard full of pain.
A troubled mind tortured by blame.
The demons came and drove me insane.
They took my soul and gave me shame.

Through the thistles and bloody thorns.
Through the desolation and destruction.
Then the faker and the crown he adorns.
He laughs, he mocks he is corruption.

Then the sun shines on this flower
For a single rose a ray of hope.
From gods heaven this light empowers.
It gives this flower the strength to cope.

You And Me

As all the Saints ride up on high,
On mighty horses through the sky,
Look down on man's plight and sigh,
At a planet that is about to die.

Mankind has made a decision,
To ignore the signs that are given,
When all is there and plain to see,
No one cares that's you and me.

There still is time to turn this about,
Everyone has to march and shout,
Stop thinking about your worth,
Now is the time to save the earth.

And if the Saints did ride up on high.
On mighty horses through the sky.
Look down on man's plight and sigh.
They Might just ride right on by.

The Bitch

You think you are so beautiful,
You think you are so chic,
You think you are so wonderful,
The girl everyone wants to meet.

You walk about the office with a smile,
You really do like to please,
You always go the extra mile,
You do this with consummate ease,

You try to take the lead,
You like to impress,
The girl that everyone needs,
But you really couldn't care less.

You're the one who volunteers,
For every mundane task,
Making sure everyone hears,
That you do everything you're asked,

At the Christmas party,
You want all the attention,
The main attraction wanting to be seen,
Looking for a reaction, a deva a queen.

Money is no problem,
You've gone through life without a hitch
For your Daddy he is rich,
As for you you're a supercilious bitch,

I only ever wanted to be a poet

As I sit here and contemplate I glance at
The clock and know I'm going to be late,
again.
You see I have a job pulling levers
and pushing knobs,
A puller and a pusher is what I am.
Not a mover nor a shaker.
Not baker nor a cabinet maker.
I dream a lot I dream about righting
the wrongs then my mind wonders
and it starts to ponder about words
and music tea and biscuits, long
legged ladies in leotards and tights.
Then I come to and I've wronged all
the rights.
Endeavour is my name endeavouring
is my game.
Before I was a puller and a pusher
I was a meeter and a greeter.
Then a gamekeepers beater.
I worked in a store,
opening and shutting doors.
I worked down the market
flogging carpets.
My endeavouring knows no bounds.
And I know you wouldn't know it.
But all I ever wanted to be is a poet.

The Poppy

I wish my Daddy was not a poppy
I wish my Daddy was home with me
He went away on a big grey boat all
across the sea. He never said how long
he was going to be. He wrote me a letter
my Mummy read to me.

Dear Princess,
I love you so much, I miss
your lovely smile and the little curls in
your hair. I miss the look you give when
you're determined to be heard. I miss our
bedtime stories, the one about the fairy
in Neverland and little Bo Peep that makes
you fall asleep. I miss our little walks with
Mummy through the fields and then to
Nellie Dixons for a cup of tea and a cake.
But most of all I miss our little home that
you and Mummy make.
It's time for me to go to work now, God
Bless Princess and give Mummy a kiss from
me and don't get all soppy.

Love Daddy.

I wish my Daddy was not a poppy.
I wish my Daddy was home with me.

The Spandau Nag

Cannonade pound all through the night
Phosphorus exploding burning bright
Rat a Tat Tat the Spandau Nag
Another thousand corpses in a bag.

Soldiers line up in the pouring rain
Waiting for the signal to go again
The soldiers know this is insane
Another thousand died in vain.

Come on boys we have to do better
So sit down and write your last letter
It's over the top again tomorrow
Into the corpse infested horror.

The generals are impervious to the death
They just tut tut with whisky breath
All they did was plan the barrage
With no concern for the carnage.

So off they went again at dawn
All in a line bayonets drawn
Rat a Tat Tat the Spandau Nag
Sixty thousand corpses in a bag.

39 Scars

The guns stopped we heard the silence then the
screams, the acrid smoke slowly cleared and there
before us the utter depravity of war unfolded.
The enemy trench 1,000 yards 10,000 breaths to
walk into death. Cold sweat like acid stinging.
The smell of fear and loose bowels a muttered
prayer thoughts of home a tear.
The Whistle blew 5,000 men walked in line
Through the pockedmarked landscape
painted in blood, to kill or be killed.
Leaving god behind.
The thump of the mortar bombs ripping the
killing ground, machine guns shedding the line.
The officer stops, he turns then dies. One of
two thousand that will be forever dead.
11th of November 1956.
The boy stands and watches as the red poppies
Are laid by his father, just twenty Lancashire
Loyals stood proud holding back the tears.
They marched away the boys father favouring
his left side, the boy knew why 39 scars up his
left side.
The officer stopped turned then died
Enabling the boys father to survive.
Thirty nine scars I counted them.
I was that boy.
In memory of Private Francis William Walmsley.

www.ingramcontent.com/pod-product-compliance
Ingram Content Group UK Ltd.
Pitfield, Milton Keynes, MK11 3LW, UK
UKHW041643190726
13854UKWH00006B/2665

9 781789 558760